HANDLING STRESS AND EMOTIONS:

Guide on how to handle your stress and master your emotion

Walter D.kerns

Table of contents

Chapter 1

what are stress and emotions

Stress is our body's response to pressure. Many different situations or life events can cause stress. It is often triggered when we experience something new, unexpected or that threatens our sense of self, or when we feel we have little control over a situation.

We all deal with stress differently. Our ability to cope can depend on our genetics, early life events, personality and social and economic circumstances.

When we encounter stress, our body produces stress hormones that trigger a fight or flight response and activate our immune system. This helps us respond quickly to dangerous situations.

Sometimes, this stress response can be useful: it can help us push through fear or pain so we can run a marathon or deliver a speech, for example. Our stress hormones will usually go back to normal quickly once the stressful event is over, and there won't be any lasting effects.

However, too much stress can cause negative effects. It can leave us in a permanent stage of fight or flight, leaving us overwhelmed or unable to cope. Long term, this can affect our physical and mental health.

Individuals may encounter a variety of stress events in daily life. If those events are disposed of inappropriately, there will be a high probability of producing a series of negative consequences. Findings from previous studies have shown that psychological stress responses often include negative emotions. In other words, people experience a complex array of negative emotions, such as depression, anxiety, anger, and distress during real-life stressful events.

Those negative emotions may potentially lead to poorer health outcomes and subsequent increased risk of complications a decreased quality of life and increased health care usage

Many studies have discussed the relationship between stress and negative emotions. However, understanding the mechanisms of stress associated with negative emotions is critical, as it has the potential to provide an opportunity for those in stress to reduce their negative emotions. The current study aims to investigate the association between stress and negative emotions in a daily-life context, and further to explore the potential mechanism by considering the role of rumination.

Stress and Negative Emotions

Stress is defined as a relationship between individuals and environment that is appraised as personally significant and as taxing or exceeding resources for coping. According to Stress and coping theory a framework is provided to test hypotheses about the stress process and its relation to physical and mental health. Certain emotions like anger, shame, and anxiety usually arise from stress, which refers to harmful, threatening, or challenging conditions, showing a relationship between stress and emotion. Based on Lazarus and Folkman's theory stress and emotion depend on how an individual evaluates transactions with the environment. During the appraisal, when people find something significant to themselves is uncontrollable, they tend to feel high levels of stress.

In terms of the relationship between stress and negative emotions, researchers have reached a consensus that they are closely associated with each other. For instance, some researchers found that depression is a form of stress response and found that stress can positively predict anxiety symptoms. What's more, a study on 5236 college students found that the higher level of stress on learning, interpersonal relationships and other issues they are facing, the more likely they are to show angry emotions. Another study on 939 American teenagers also reported that individuals' perceived stress positively predicts their anger, which in turn affects their misbehavior, such as substance use . Also, the perceived stress in cancer patients indicated a significant positive correlation to anger and depression

However, most previous studies have used questionnaires as a measure method. Retrospective and heuristic biases of traditional assessment instruments are known to systematically distort recollections of past experiences and events. To minimize them, Ambulatory Assessment (AA) was recently raised. AA is a method used to repeated sampling of thoughts, feelings, or behaviors as close in time to the experience as possible in the naturalistic environment It can provide real-time (or near real-time) assessments and create more stable estimates of phenomena that fluctuate over time compared to single time-point measurement

As mentioned above, appraisals in the stress process generate emotions that vary in quality and intensity, and numerous studies proved the association between stress and negative emotions. However, few of them examined the cognitive style as the mechanism in this relationship. Rumination, as one of the most typical negative cognitive styles, will be explored to investigate its role in the relationship between stress and negative emotions.

It is demonstrated by Nolen-Hoeksema, that rumination in response to stress is associated concurrently with depressive symptoms. Many researchers believed that information processing impairments contribute to ruminative tendencies , when individuals encounter stress, cognitive control impairments may contribute to higher levels of rumination. Another study has similar conclusion that rumination is a common response to stress in adolescence In an experimental study, Smith and Alloy found that individuals' rumination was reactive to their perceived stress

The Current Study

Since rumination is a main indicator of negative emotions and can also be predicted by stress, it is probable that rumination acts as a mediator in the relationship between stress and negative emotion. This mediation model will be tested in the current study. Individuals with higher perceived stress may have more rumination and more negative emotions in daily life, and more rumination would predict increased negative emotional responses.

As mentioned above, to eliminate the retrospective and heuristic biases of self-report questionnaires and investigate the dynamic relations between different variables, we adopted AA to gather individuals' data of stress, rumination, and negative emotions. In line with previous research and theory, we predicted that stress and negative emotions would be associated over time. We hypothesized that (1) stress at time t predicts subsequent state negative emotions at time t+1 in daily life, (2) state rumination is positively associated with state negative emotions at time t, and (3) rumination is a mediator of the association between the relationship of stress and negative emotions at both within-person and between-person levels.Stress was assessed by two questions: "Do you feel nervous and stress at the moment?", and "Do you have the feeling that you can't control the important things in your life?". Item was rated on a 7-point Likert scale ranging from 0 ("not at all") to 6 ("very much so"). Higher score indicates a higher level of stress. Items assessed one's feeling of stress at that moment. The questionnaire had good internal consistency reliability in the current sample, with a Cronbach's alpha .

Negative emotions were assessed with three items assessing depression, anger, and anxiety respectively (e.g. "Do you feel angry at the moment?"). Items were rated on a 7-point Likert scale ranging from 0 ("not at all") to 6 ("very much so"). Higher scores indicate high level of negative affect

Chapter 2

what are the nature of stress and emotions

Stress problems are very common. The American Psychological Association's 2007 "Stress in America" poll found that one-third of people in the United States report experiencing extreme levels of negative stress. In addition, nearly one out of five people report that they are experiencing high levels of negative stress 15 or more days per month. Impressive as these figures are, they represent only a cross-section of people's stress levels at one particular moment of their lives. When stress is considered as something that occurs repeatedly across the full lifespan, the true incidence of stress problems is much higher. Being "stressed out" is thus a universal human phenomenon that affects almost everyone.

What are we talking about when we discuss stress? Generally, most people use the word stress to refer to negative experiences that leave us feeling overwhelmed. Thinking about stress exclusively as something negative gives us a false impression of its true nature, however. Stress is a reaction to a changing, demanding environment. Properly considered, stress is really more about our capacity to handle change than it is about whether that change makes us feel good or bad. Change happens all the time, and stress is in large part what we feel when we are reacting to it.

We can define stress by saying that it involves the "set of emotional, physical, and cognitive (i.e., thought) reactions to a change." Thinking about stress as a reaction to change suggests that it is not necessarily bad, and sometimes, could even be a good thing. Some life changes such as getting a new job, moving in with a new romantic partner, or studying to master a new skill are generally considered positive and life-enhancing events, even though they can also be quite stressful. Other life changes such as losing a job or an important relationship are more negative, and also stressful.

Our experience of stress varies in intensity between high and low. How intensely stressed we feel in response to a particular event has to do with how much we need to accomplish in order to meet the demands of that situation. When we don't have to do much in order to keep up with demands, we don't experience much stress. Conversely, when we have to do a lot, we tend to feel much more stressed out.

Generally speaking, people do not like experiencing the extremes of stress. This is true for each end of the spectrum of stress intensity, both high and low. Few people enjoy the feeling of being overwhelmingly stressed in the face of great change.

However, most people do not like a total absence of stress either, at least after a while. There is a word for such a condition (i.e., a lack of stress and challenge) which conveys this negative meaning: boredom. What most people tend to seek is the middle ground; a balance between a lack of stress and too much stress. They want a little challenge and excitement in life, but not so much that they feel overwhelmed by it.

A variety of events and environmental demands cause us to experience stress, including: routine hassles (such as getting the family out the door in the morning, or dealing with a difficult co-worker), one-time events that alter our lives (such as moving, marriage, childbirth, or changing jobs), and ongoing long-term demands (such as dealing with a chronic disease, or caring for a child or sick family member). Though different people may experience the same type of events, each of them will experience that event in a unique way. That is, some people are more vulnerable to becoming stressed out than others are in any given situation. An event like getting stuck in traffic might cause one person to become very stressed out while it might not affect another person much at all. Even "good" stressors such as getting married can impact individuals differently. Some people become highly anxious while others remain calm and composed.

How vulnerable you are personally to becoming stressed out depends on a variety of factors, including your biological makeup; your perception of your ability to cope with challenges; characteristics of the stressful event (e.g., the "stressor") such as it's intensity, timing, and duration; and your command of stress management skills. While some of these factors (such as your genetics and often, the characteristics of the stressor itself) are not under your direct control, some of the other factors are.

what causes stress and emotion

Emotional distress is a state of emotional sufferingTrusted Source. The term encompasses a wide range of symptoms, but its hallmarks are the symptoms of depression and anxiety. People can experience it at any time, and it is usually temporary.

Mental health disorders can cause symptoms of emotional distress that persist for long periods or occur in cycles.

The symptoms of emotional distress are sometimes severe and may develop into a mental health disorder.

Some symptoms of emotional distress include:

feeling overwhelmed, helpless, or hopeless
feeling guilty without a clear cause
spending a lot of time worrying
having difficulty thinking or remembering
sleeping too much or too little
having changes in appetite
relying more heavily on mood-altering substances, such as alcohol
isolating from people or activities
experiencing unusual anger or irritability

experiencing fatigue

having difficulty keeping up with daily tasks

experiencing new, unexplainedThe causes of emotional distress vary widely, and they usually involve a combination of factors.

For some people, distress is due to a traumatic experience or event, such as a death in the family. It can also result from a wide range of underlying mental health conditions.

In other cases, certain situations trigger emotional distress. We give examples of these situations below:

Emotional distress at work

The workplace can be a stressful environment, and while some stress may be motivating, too much is often overwhelming.

Some causes of emotional distress related to work may include:

concerns about job security
concerns about performance
long hours
low pay
poor working conditions
increasing responsibility
a lack of control over work
relationships with colleagues or managers

Sometimes, circumstances build and combine in unexpected ways to cause distress. A person can experience this in any workplace and at all levels of an organization.

Long working hours may be a particularly potent cause of emotional distress. For example, an older studyTrusted Source from 2011 found that people working more than 55 hours a week were more likely to experience depression and anxiety in the future than those working 35–40 hours per week.

Emotional distress at home

Among the many possible causes of emotional distress at home are personal or environmental factors, such as:

experiencing relationship problems with partners, other family members, or friends

undergoing major life changes, such as moving home or having a child

living in a neighborhood that faces inequity and a deprivation of resources

having a low income

experiencing discrimination

feeling lonely or isolated

having debt

having an unhealthful lifestyle, which might involve smoking or low levels of exercise

Emotional distress is a broad term. It can refer to a wide range of symptoms from a variety of mental health disorders, but many people without any disorders experience it.

Whether or not a mental health problem is present, emotional distress can be overwhelming and affect daily functioning.

The symptoms may resolve on their own, but a variety of strategies can help, such as practicing stress reduction and building a support network.

If the symptoms of emotional distress are persistent or hard to manage, a person should contact a doctor or mental health professional.

Chapter 3

How to manage your stress and emotions

Fortunately, while you can't always fix these situations overnight, you can lessen the emotional stress you feel, and the toll this stress takes on you. Here are some exercises you can try to effectively cope with emotional stress.

stress management techniques

Causes of Emotional Stress

Coping With Emotional Stress

Emotional stress can be particularly painful and be challenging to deal with. It can take more of a toll than many other forms of stress. Part of the reason is that thinking about a solution, or discussing solutions with a good friend—coping behaviors that are often useful and effective in solving problems—can easily deteriorate into rumination and co-rumination, which are not so useful and effective.

In fact, rumination can exacerbate your stress levels, so it helps to have healthy strategies for coping with emotional stress as well as redirecting yourself away from rumination and avoidance coping and more toward emotionally proactive approaches to stress management.

Causes of Emotional Stress

Relationship stress carries a heavy toll on our emotional lives and creates strong emotional responses. Our relationships greatly impact our lives— or better or for worse.

Healthy relationships can bring good times, but also resources in times of need, added resilience in times of stress, and even increased longevity. However, conflicted relationships and 'frenemies' can make us worse off in our emotional lives, and can even take a toll physically.

Relationships aren't the only cause of emotional stress, however. Financial crises, an unpleasant work environment, or a host of other stressors can cause emotional stress, which sometimes tempts us toward unhealthy coping behaviors in order to escape the pain, especially when the situations seem hopeless.

Perhaps one of the more challenging aspects of coping with emotional stress is the feeling of being unable to change the situation. If we can't change our stress levels by eliminating the stressful situation, we can work on our emotional response to it.

Coping With Emotional Stress
Fortunately, while you can't always fix these situations overnight, you can lessen the emotional stress you feel, and the toll this

stress takes on you. Here are some exercises you can try to effectively cope with emotional stress.

Practice Mindfulness

When we feel emotional stress, it's also often experienced as physical pain. You may feel a 'heavy' feeling in the chest, an unsettled feeling in the stomach, a dull headache.

It's common to try to escape these feelings, but it can actually be helpful to go deeper into the experience and use mindfulness to really notice where these emotional responses are felt physically. Some people notice that the pain seems more intense before dissipating, but then they feel the emotional and physical pain is lessened.

Distract Yourself

Common belief used to be that if we didn't express every emotion we felt (or at least the big ones), they would show themselves in other ways. In some ways, this is true. There are benefits to examining our emotional states to learn from what our emotions are trying to tell us, and 'stuffing our emotions' in unhealthy ways can bring other problems.

However, it's also been discovered that distracting oneself from emotional pain with emotionally healthy alternatives—such as a feel-good movie, fun activities with friends, or a satisfying mental challenge—can lessen emotional pain and help us feel better.

How to Cope With Emotions Using Distraction

Block Off Some Time

If you find that emotional stress and rumination creep into your awareness quite a bit, and distraction doesn't work, try scheduling some time—an hour a day, perhaps—where you allow yourself to think about your situation fully and mull over solutions, concoct hypothetical possibilities, replay upsetting exchanges, or whatever you feel the emotional urge to do.

Journaling is a great technique to try here, especially if it's done as both an exploration of your inner emotional world and an exploration of potential solutions. Talk to your friends about the problem, if you'd like. Fully immerse yourself. And then try some healthy distractions.

This technique works well for two reasons. First, if you really have the urge to obsess, this allows you to satisfy that craving in a limited context. Also, you may find yourself more relaxed the rest of the day because you know that there will be a time to focus on your emotional situation; that time is just later.

Practice Meditation

Meditation is very helpful for dealing with a variety of stressors, and emotional stress is definitely in the category of stressors that meditation helps with. It allows you to take a break from rumination by actively redirecting your thoughts, and provides practice in choosing thoughts, which can help eliminate some emotional stress in the long term.

5 Meditation Techniques to Get You Started

Talk to a Therapist

If you find your level of emotional stress interfering with your daily activities or threatening your well-being in other ways, you may consider seeing a therapist for help working through emotional issues. Whatever the cause of your emotional stress, you can work toward lessening and managing it and feeling better in the process, without losing the 'messages' that your emotions are bringing you.

If you or a loved one are struggling with stress, contact the Substance Abuse
Stress is a natural reaction to difficult situations in life, such as work, family, relationships and money problems.

We mentioned earlier that a moderate amount of stress can help us perform better in challenging situations, but too much or prolonged stress can lead to physical problems. This can include lower immunity levels, digestive and intestinal difficulties such as irritable bowel syndrome (IBS), or mental health problems such as depression. It is therefore important that we manage our stress and keep it at a healthy level to prevent long-term damage to our bodies and minds.

When you are feeling stressed, try to take these steps:

• Realize when it is causing you a problem. You need to make the connection between feeling tired or ill, with the pressures you are faced with. Do not ignore physical warnings such as tense muscles, over-tiredness, headaches or migraines.

• Identify the causes. Try to identify the underlying causes. Sort the possible reasons for your stress into those with a practical solution, those that will get better anyway given time, and those you can't do anything about. Try to let go of those in the second and third groups – there is no point in worrying about things you can't change or things that will sort themselves out.

• Review your lifestyle. Are you taking on too much? Are there things you are doing which could be handed over to someone else? Can you do things in a more leisurely way? You may need to prioritize things you are trying to achieve and reorganize your life so that you are not trying to do everything at once.

You can also help protect yourself from stress in a number of ways:

• Eat healthily. A healthy diet will reduce the risks of diet-related diseases. Also, there is a growing amount of evidence showing how food affects our mood. Feelings of wellbeing can be protected by ensuring that our diet provides adequate amounts of brain nutrients such as essential vitamins and minerals, as well as water.

• Be aware of your smoking and drinking. Even though they may seem to reduce tension, this is misleading as they often make problems worse.

• Exercise. Physical exercise can be very effective in relieving stress. Even going out to get some fresh air and doing some light physical exercise, like walking to the shops, can help.

• Take time out. Take time to relax. Saying 'I just can't take the time off' is no use if you are forced to take time off later through ill health. Striking a balance between responsibility to others and responsibility to yourself is vital in reducing stress levels.

• Be mindful. Mindfulness meditation can be practiced anywhere at any time. Research has suggested that it can reduce the effects of stress, anxiety and other related problems such as insomnia, poor concentration and low moods, in some people. Our 'Be Mindful' website features a specially-developed online course in mindfulness, as well as details of local courses in your area: bemindful.co.uk

• Get some restful sleep. Sleeping problems are common when you're suffering from stress. Try to ensure you get enough rest. For more tips on getting a good night's sleep read our guide 'How to...sleep better' at: mentalhealth.org.uk/howto

• Don't be too hard on yourself. Try to keep things in perspective. After all, we all have bad days

Chapter 4

How to use emotions and stress to grow

Stress can also be an opportunity for growth

First you need to adopt a "stress is beneficial" mindset

Then you need to take action on something important to you

During times of crisis, it's not unusual to worry about things that feel out of your control. In the current pandemic, many of us are concerned about matters of health, finances and even whether to send our kids back to school. You might be worrying about what long-term effects there could be for yourself, your team, or your family.

These worries can lead to feelings of anxiety and stress.

For some, they might lead to long-term problems such as post-traumatic stress disorder, which is a condition of persistent mental and emotional stress.

But what about those individuals who come through difficult periods and experience growth afterward? This phenomenon is called post-traumatic growth. How is it that these individuals come through the trauma with a positive response? And, even more importantly, how can more of us experience this?

The theory of post-traumatic growth was developed by psychologists Richard Tedeschi and Lawrence Calhoun. They found that for individuals who grew after a trauma, they saw improved relationships, greater appreciation of life, and enhanced perceptions of strength and mastery.

So what determines whether stress and trauma will harm or help us? It turns out that . . . we do.

There are two tools that can help us leverage the stress we're feeling and turn it into a growth opportunity. The first is our mindset and the second is our actions.

Let's first look at mindsets. There is a considerable body of research regarding the effectiveness of mindset changes as it relates to post-traumatic growth. When we push ourselves to modify how we're thinking about a situation, it can change our results. In this way, our mindset about stress can become a self-fulfilling prophecy.

Stress can activate a variety of responses. When we adopt a "stress-is-beneficial" mindset, however, we're far more likely to achieve an optimal level of activation. In other words, we are energized enough to take action but not too much as to find it paralyzing or overwhelming.

I have been using this simple but powerful tool with my clients over the last several months. While we acknowledge the stress they feel, I ask them to rephrase how they are thinking about the situation so that they are seeing it as an opportunity rather than as a threat.

It's not about saying "This isn't stressful." But it is about telling ourselves "Stress can also be good for me" or "I have what it takes to manage this situation." In many cases, we explore together what strengths they already have that will serve them well for upcoming challenges.

Now that we've looked at the mindset, let's consider the actions we can take. The first action is to take care of yourself. You might use this as an opportunity to explore better methods of self-care or recommit to healthful practices like getting sufficient sleep, eating the right foods, and getting more exercise. When we tend to our own needs, we have more resources available to deal with the situation and continue to look forward.

In addition to caring for yourself, it is the time to take action on something important to you; find one thing you can do to move yourself forward, and it can quickly decrease your negative feelings. This could be reconnecting with someone in your network, getting clear on your career goals and aspirations or tackling a task you have been putting off. Making progress on meaningful work keeps us focused on our goals.

We know we can't always control the circumstances we're in, but we do have the opportunity to consider how we respond to them. When faced with stress and trauma, it's important to acknowledge your stress and the corresponding emotions you feel — and then see that stress as a resource you can leverage to achieve your goals.

We can acknowledge the situations and challenges around us. We don't pretend they aren't happening or that they don't have any negative effects. But then we ask ourselves: "What's next?"

It's about seeing stress and trauma as challenging, rather than threatening. It's about acknowledging that the current situation is the beginning — rather than the end.

All Emotions Are Natural

Let's say you start to brainstorm a list of all the emotions you've ever experienced. Just for fun, try it now.

What's on your list? Chances are, you included things like happy, sad, excited, angry, afraid, grateful, proud, scared, confused, stressed, relaxed, amazed. Now sort your list into two categories — positive emotions and negative emotions.

Feeling both positive and negative emotions is a natural part of being human. We might use the word "negative" to describe more difficult emotions, but it doesn't mean those emotions are bad or we shouldn't have them. Still, most people would probably rather feel a positive emotion than a negative one. It's likely you'd prefer to feel happy instead of sad, or confident instead of insecure.

What matters is how our emotions are balanced — how much of each type of emotion, positive or negative, we experience.

How Negative Emotions Help Us
Negative emotions warn us of threats or challenges that we may need to deal with. For example, fear can alert us to possible danger. It's a signal that we might need to protect ourselves. Angry feelings warn us that someone is stepping on our toes, crossing a boundary, or violating our trust. Anger can be a signal that we might need to act on our own behalf.

Negative emotions focus our awareness. They help us to zero in on a problem so we can deal with it. But too many negative emotions can make us feel overwhelmed, anxious, exhausted, or stressed out. When negative emotions are out of balance, problems might seem too big to handle.

The more we dwell on negative emotions, the more negative we begin to feel. Focusing on negativity just keeps it going.

How Positive Emotions Help Us
Positive emotions balance out negative ones, but they have other powerful benefits, too.

Instead of narrowing our focus like negative emotions do, positive emotions affect our brains in ways that increase our awareness, attention, and memory. They help us take in more information, hold several ideas in mind at once, and understand how different ideas relate to each other.

When positive emotions open us up to new possibilities, we are more able to learn and build on our skills. That leads to doing better on tasks and tests.

People who have plenty of positive emotions in their everyday lives tend to be happier, healthier, learn better, and get along well with others.

The Importance of Positive Emotions
Science is helping us find out how valuable positive emotions can be. Experts have learned a lot from recent brain studies. Here are two findings that can help us use positive emotions to our advantage:

1. Let Positive Emotions Outnumber Negative Ones
When we feel more positive emotions than negative ones, difficult situations are easier to handle. Positive emotions build our resilience (the emotional resources needed for coping). They broaden our awareness, letting us see more options for problem solving.

Studies show that people feel and do their best when they have at least three times as many positive emotions as negative emotions. That's because of something called the negativity bias.

The negativity bias is a natural human tendency to pay more attention to negative emotions than to positive ones. It makes sense when you think about it: Negative emotions call our attention to problems — problems we might need to deal with quickly. Tuning in to negative emotions can be a survival mechanism.

badly, not well, even if we experienced equal amounts of positive and emotions that day. It takes at least three times as many positive emotions to tip the scales and make a day seem like a great one.

2. Practice Positivity Every Day

Building habits that encourage us to feel more positive emotions can help us be happier, do better, and reduce our negative emotions. Building positive emotions is especially important if we're already dealing with a lot of negative feelings such as fear, sadness, anger, frustration, or stress.

Building a daily positivity habit is pretty simple. It comes down to two basic steps:

Notice and name your positive emotions. Start by simply focusing on your feelings. You can tune in to your emotions in real time, as they happen. Or take stock at the end of the day, noting how you felt in different situations. For example, you might feel proud when you answer a question right, joyful when your puppy chases you around the yard, or loved when your mom shows up at your game.

When you first start doing this, you'll probably need to remind yourself to focus on your emotions. But — like any habit — it gets easier the more you do it.

Pick an emotion and act to increase it. Let's say you choose confidence: What helps you feel confident? How can you get more of that feeling? You might give yourself a "Yes, I can!" pep talk before a test. Or maybe you stand up straighter and practice walking through the halls in a confident way, feeling strong and powerful.

Positive emotions feel good, and they're good for you. Pay attention to these powerful tools and find ways to make time for them in your everyday life. Create room in your day for joy, fun, friendship, relaxation, gratitude, and kindness. Make these things a habit and you will positively be happier you!